The Rising Son

Written and Illustrated by Chloe Bambrick

Text and illustrations copyright © 2013 and 2017 by Chloe Bambrick. All rights reserved. No part of this publication may be reproduced or transmitted in any form by any means, electronic or mechanical, including photocopy, recording, or on any informational storage and retrieval system, without permission in writing from the author, Chloe Bambrick.

Requests for permission to make copies of any part of the work should be sent to: bambric423@gmail.com

Library of Congress Cataloging in Publishing Data

Bambrick, Chloe, Author and Illustrator

The Rising Son

Summary: **The Rising Son** tells the story of a young lion cub on a quest to become a strong grownup like his parents. Watch him change and grow as he learns a few life lessons on how giving to others can lead to a beautiful existence.

[1. Growing up to adulthood. 2. Helping others. 3. Community volunteering. 4. African Lions.]

ISBN: 978-0-9992760-0-6 (paperback)

Typesetting, Composition, Digital Imaging: Rosanna I. Porter, Raisykinder Publishing.

This book is dedicated to ...

My late friend Mary Lonowski who was a beautiful, giving, and dedicated person as well as a servant to her community. Her family and the entire community loved her deeply and have missed her every day since her passing. I hope this story inspires children to be kind, giving, helpful, and love others the way that Mary did.

To my loving parents, Dale and Cathy, and my sister Taneum. I would be nowhere without you and I will always appreciate the love and support you have given me.

Chloe Bambrick

From the savanna I was born.
From the savanna I am.
From my mother I was born.
A lion I am.

A small lion I am.
A big lion I should be.
My parents are unlike me.
How could that be?

My Father is big.
My Father can hunt.
My Father is HUGE.
I feel like a runt!

My Mother is so brave.
My Mother is so kind.
My Mother is so graceful.
Why am I always on
my behind?

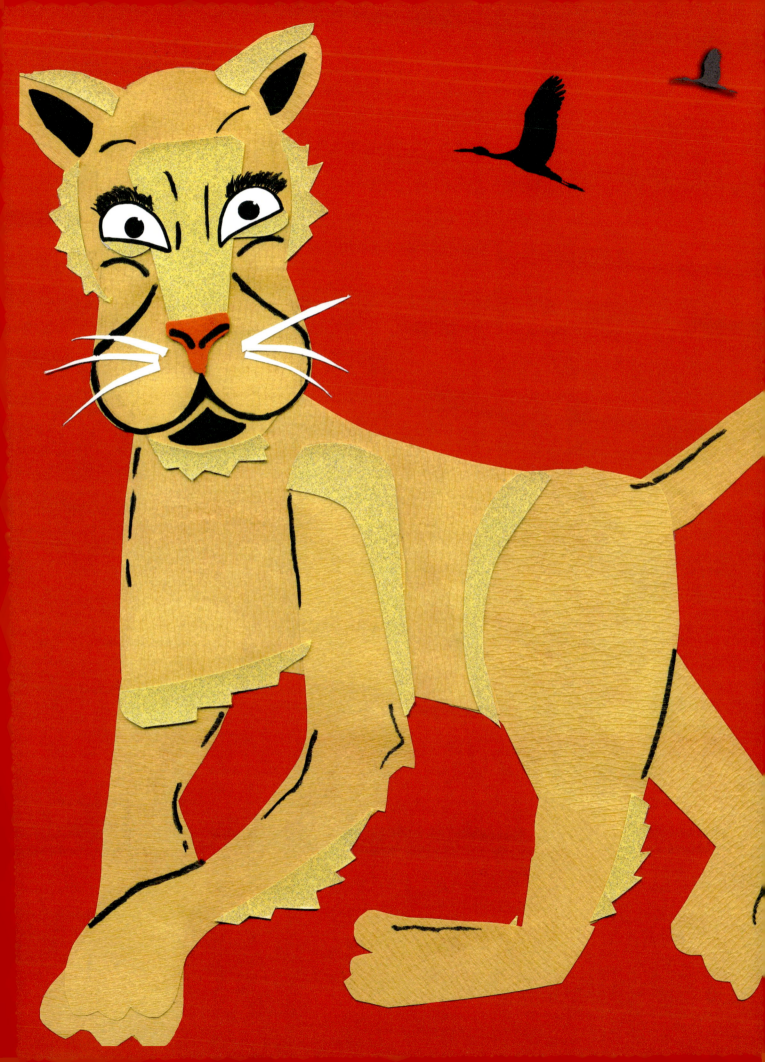

Father when will I have
a mane like yours?
Father when will I have a roar?
Mother when will I stop
tripping on my feet?
Mother why I am I always
so sore?

Son, to grow this mane
I had to work.
Growing this mane was a chore.
I would never have grown
this mane if I had always
wished for more.

When you learn this valuable lesson son,
you will grow.
When you learn this valuable lesson son,
your mane will show.
When your mane begins to show,
your roar will finally soar.
And on your feet you can run
because your growing will be done.
You will not be sore, no, not any more.

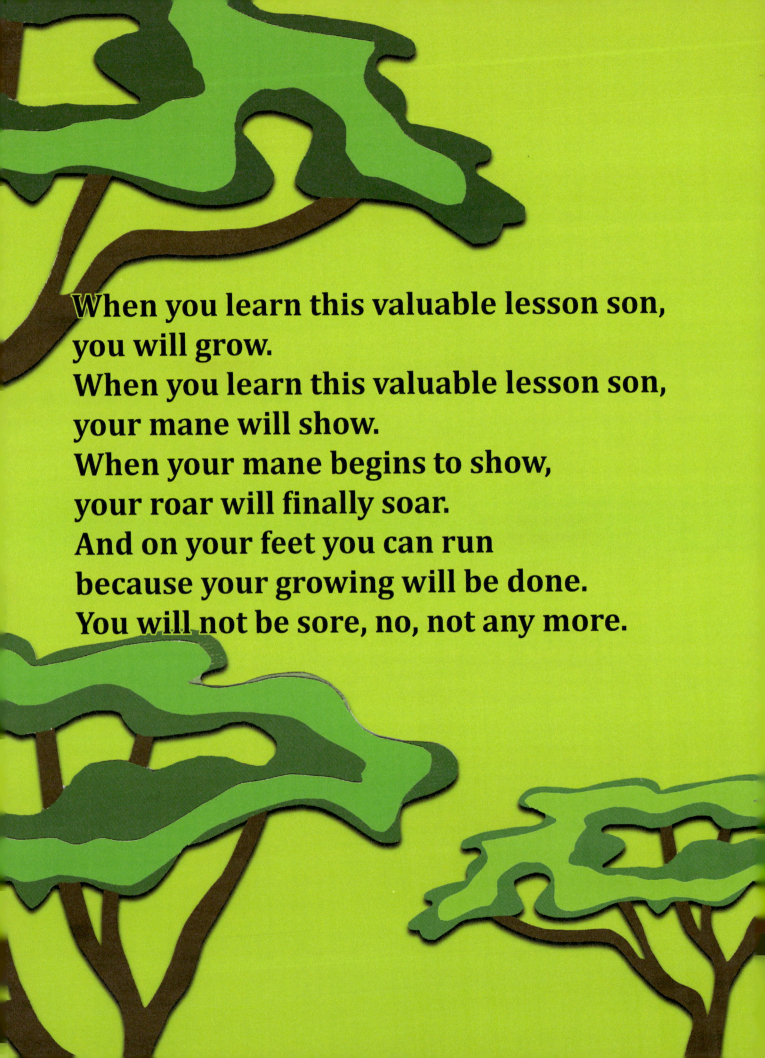

To learn this valuable lesson
will take time.
Like my parents,
I will learn this lesson
through hard work.
If I am to grow up
big and strong,
I will have to help others
get along.

Helping is fun.
Helping is good.
Mrs. Giraffe couldn't reach the leaves in the trees, but with me she could.

I grabbed all of the leaves with one big pull.
So, at the end of the day she would feel full.

Mr. Rhino was thirsty.
Mr. Rhino was lost.
He asked me for directions
because he thought
he may have turned
left instead of right.
With my help, I led him to water.
The thirst was gone for
both he and his daughter.

Ms. Crocodile had a loose tooth.
A problem she could not fix.
I tied a string around her tooth,
and counted to six!
With my help, we got it loose.
She was happy to have her mouth back in use.

Mr. Elephant was scared.
He was afraid of mice.
It seemed that no one cared.
With my help Mr. Elephant was free,
because I asked the mice to leave him be.

From helping others I learned
a valuable lesson.
From helping I have grown.
After taking my parents advice,
a new side of me has shown.

This mane I grew
came from work.
This mane I grew
came from helping.

By growing this mane
I learned a lesson.
I shouldn't want more.
I should always want to give
and help others soar.

The End

Made in the USA
San Bernardino, CA
03 August 2017